Promises of **Bipolar**

A BIOGRAPHY OF BRUCE MONK

Murray Bruce Monk

PROMISES OF BIPOLAR
A BIOGRAPHY OF BRUCE MONK

iUniverse books may be ordered through booksellers or by contacting:

iUniverse
1663 Liberty Drive
Bloomington, IN 47403
www.iuniverse.com
1-800-Authors (1-800-288-4677)

ISBN: 978-1-5320-2946-2 (sc)
ISBN: 978-1-5320-2947-9 (e)

Library of Congress Control Number: 2017913767

Print information available on the last page.

iUniverse rev. date: 03/16/2018

My name is Murray Bruce Monk. I was born on a farm in Musquodoboit, which is in Wyses Corner, Halifax County, Nova Scotia. I lived with my grandparents.

When I was just a little boy, my grandmother and grandfather would take me on an hour-and-a-half walk down to the river to go fishing in my grandfather's rowboat. We would have to put lotion on our arms and faces so the mosquitoes wouldn't bite. The rowboat held six people.

I would cut down branches to make fishing poles for my grandfather and me, and my grandmother and I would buy fly hooks and other hooks for my grandfather. When I went to town, where my brother and sister lived, I would dig worms to put on the fishhooks, and we would use lots of them for fishing. I would cut and clean the trout we caught and then would cut off their heads so we could cook them in the frying pan with lots of butter, which my grandmother made at home.

There was a large field on the right side of the house. My grandfather had a riding lawn mower and a gas can for a Sport Sony SWL, which was way too small for the big lawn mower. The blades were twelve feet long on each side. He'd also had a black workhorse called Dick before he could afford to buy the lawn mower. When we did the second field below the house, we made two thousand bales of hay. It took days and days until we got all the hay into the barn.

As a little boy I would watch my grandfather make hay in the barn. When haying season was ready, I would climb up on top of the wagon and tramp down the hay. There would be pulleys attached to the barn up high and two large forks that would dig into the hay bales on top of the wagon. They would be lifted up and go into the barn. When the horse went forward, a bale of hay was lifted into the barn. Someone would pull a rope, and the hay would fall to the bottom of the barn until the barn was full. We did the same thing with the straw. The straw was used for the animals to sleep on and to keep them warm in the winter.

As a boy, I used to kill green snakes and try to catch baby frogs and toads. I wandered around looking for green snakes to kill with my pitchfork. My grandfather had two oxen, but I forget what he used them for.

My grandparents had twenty cows, thirty chickens, a rooster, twenty pigs, a collie dog, a cat, and Dick, the black workhorse. The farm was sixty miles from Halifax. My grandfather would put the cows in the barn at about three o'clock in the afternoon, and the collie would help round them up. My grandfather would milk nineteen cows, and I would milk one. The horse would drink a bucket of water every suppertime; we would give the horse a bucket of water and then be done for the day by six o'clock in the evening.

I followed my grandfather everywhere. I fed pigs, chickens, cattle, horses, a dog, and a cat.

One time I went to feed the chickens and then reached under the hens to get their eggs. One of the hens bit me and left a scar, which I still have today. After that, I didn't feed them or even visit the henhouse for a week, but I didn't tell my grandfather or grandmother this. I remember my grandfather borrowed two glass tanks. There were eight layers and newborn chickens. I think he got the tanks because I didn't feed them for a week.

During the winter months my grandfather took me on sleigh rides in the snow. He also took us to the United Church on Sundays with the horse and sleigh.

Not far from the farmhouse was a brook that had a beaver dam. I would spend hours trying to see the beaver. I would also try to find birds' nests by the river so that I could take down the nests and look after the birds until they were big enough to fly away. I would also go searching for turtles. In addition, I helped my grandfather clean out the barn. I would take a shovel and muck out the cow stalls. Then I'd give them hay and oats to eat. I would rub down and brush the workhorse so the horse would be clean. My grandfather would also get me to clean the track behind the cattle, put the dirty hay into the wheelbarrow, and take it out to the barn.

My grandmother had a battery-operated radio that stood five feet high and was four feet wide. Every Saturday night we listened to "The Grand Ole Opry" from Wheeling, West Virginia.

I moved in from the country when I was six years old to start school. Every week I would go to town with my mother, father, older brother, and sister to the waterfront. I started school at Notting Park School and then would go to the country every weekend with my grandfather to help with the farm. Every day at school we would get a container of white or chocolate milk, as there was no welfare when I was a kid.

When I was in grade three, my mother bought me a bicycle, a two-wheeler. We went to Canadian Tire and bought mud flaps for the fenders and handgrips for the handlebars. My mother also bought streamers for the handgrips and a red light for the handlebars.

I kept myself busy with Cub Scouts and other organizations, earning lots of badges for things I had done for the church. I went to the Church of England for two years for Cub Scouts and earned all kinds of badges. My friend was the son of the church pastor.

When I was twelve years old, I used to go on the golf course and carry golf clubs around the eighteen holes. The golfers used to pay me three dollars for the day. I'd also find numerous lost golf balls in the woods, and the golfers would pay me a quarter for each ball I found. There were also three or four neighborhood friends for whom I used to babysit when I was thirteen and fourteen years old. I would earn three dollars a night babysitting.

My brother and I started working a paper route for the *Dartmouth Free Press*. He sold 387 papers, and I sold 437 papers. We both won a trip to New York on an Italian passenger liner.

When I was eleven, I joined the Boy Scouts for a year. Around this time we had a record player and a lot of records, including those by Elvis Presley, the late Hank Williams, and many more. When I was twelve years old, I attended a Hank Williams show; he died one year later. I forget how much it cost to get into the dances, which were fundraisers for the church. I used to sing along with the records on the stage along with the record player.

When I was twelve, in 1956, I joined the Royal Canadian Army Cadets. My rank was major sniper. The insignia was crossed rifles and a crown. I went to army camp at Camp Aldershot in Kentville, sixty minutes from Halifax County. When it was raining, we would go to target practice on the range with 303 rifles. We would fire at targets from five hundred feet away. I got quite a few bull's-eyes. Then we used submachine guns and 9 mm semiautomatic pistols. The range of fire for the submachine guns was three hundred feet. We would practice on the range every day for four hours, and then we'd drill for the rest of the day. We had to clean our weapons every night, and we slept in buildings and tents. When practicing drills with our rifles, we also had to learn how to use the ham radios. I was in the Royal Canadian Artillery for four years, from 1956 to 1960, and got out when I was sixteen. I then went for training in Eastern Passage, Halifax County. I would travel on the bus every Wednesday night, and the army trucks would make special trips to pick up the boys. I was in charge of recruiting young men to join the army cadets for a year. I was picked for Camp Aldershot for four years. There were thirty-three cadets per platoon, and there were three platoons, as well as an additional platoon of sixteen men in the back of the camp. During my years as an army cadet, part of the training consisted of a trim-up, which meant we had to march for long hours. On Saturday mornings I also did pistol training at the armories in Halifax. I learned first aid as well. At the end of summer we gave a show of the skills we had learned in Halifax and Dartmouth. For example, one of the skills I gained in training was that I could take apart a submachine gun and put it back together blindfolded in seven minutes. We also had to clean our weapons every day. When it rained, we didn't have to go marching, but we went to the range and learned to use a ham radio to communicate, as I mentioned previously. When I was ten, my mother bought a brand-new bicycle for my older brother, and I rode it to school when I started junior high school in grade seven. It was a long way from our house to the school, so the bicycle came in handy. I started school when I was six. I began in low grade one and then moved to high grade one before starting grade two. I failed grade eight but passed part of grade nine. I attended part of grade nine and then grade ten English. I remember riding to night school in the country from town on my bicycle. It was sixty miles one way, and I think I did it three or four times.

Before I became a member of the Church of Jesus Christ of Latter-day Saints, I went to the Salvation Army.

I sang in the choir, raising money for the church. I used to go door-to-door in those days seeking donations and raising money at Christmastime for the poor and for the church. I remember they loaned me a tuba, and I used to blow it outside of the house.

I was baptized and ordained a priest in the Mormon Church of the Church of Jesus Christ of Latter-day Saints. It took sixteen years to become a priest. When I married, I changed religions for my wife.

When I turned sixteen years old, I got my driver's license and went to a car dealer to buy a 1947 Nash. I proudly drove it home. After I brought it home, I put my foot on the brake, and the pedal went right to the floor, so I had to get someone to tow me back to the dealership. The car dealer returned the seventy-five dollars I'd paid for the car. They then offered to finance me for $265 for a 1953 Chevrolet. I drove this car for a while and then decided to sell it to my father. After I sold the Chevrolet, I bought a brand-new 1962 Pontiac Cavalier.

When I got out of Army Cadets in 1960, I worked as a carpenter's apprentice for one year. I painted fences and helped build new houses. After that job, I worked on an oil tanker with Irving Pol. I quit after two months but then went back and stayed for one year. I then got another job working at Canadian Iron in Burnside, Dartmouth. I did tack welding and operated the crane from the ground. I ran a steel plant in 1962. I also worked with my grandfather in the woods, logging. It was hard work. He had a big black workhorse. My grandfather would put three logs in the yoke, and I would use the whip on the horse's backside to get him moving. The horse would pull up beside the logging truck, and my grandfather and I would load the logs onto the truck. I would finally sit down for about half an hour for a rest until dark.

When I was twenty years old, I moved back to eastern Canada and worked for three years as a stevedore. One day I was unloading 120-pound bags of flour from one of the crates when one of the bags fell off and hit me in the back, knocking me off my feet and injuring my back. I went to a chiropractor for almost three years to help mend the injury. Although after three years of continuous treatment, I was able to return to work, I was not able to return to work on the waterfront as a stevedore anymore.

In 1963 I went to Baltimore, Maryland, and worked at Bata Shoe Company for six weeks. I then decided to enlist in the United States Army. I passed all the tests and got an A1 classification with selective service.

I was going to rent a cottage with my wife and baby, but the hide-a-bed was full of cockroaches bigger than bumblebees. So I left there for Rochester, New York, and sent my wife back to Nova Scotia. I stayed with my uncle and saved my money to rent a trailer. I then got a job and brought my wife back from Nova Scotia. I started working for a manufacturing company, making single bagging machines for farmers. Each machine had a five-pound scoop and sold for six hundred dollars. The larger machines had a ten-pound scoop and sold for $1,200. Farmers would use these machines to weigh goods. I worked for four months and was laid off during the winter. During my layoff from the manufacturing company, I got a job with the New York Railroad in a town called East Rochester. My primary job on the railroad was to sweep debris left by the welders off the tracks. My other job was to shovel snow from the railway cars. I was in the union.

After spending three and a half years in the United States, my daughter was born. She was born with heart defects, and I was very worried about whether she was going to live. Things went from bad to worse when I suffered a nervous breakdown and was admitted to Rochester General Hospital for treatment. I remained in the hospital for one month and then was transferred to Rochester State Hospital. My hospital bill was around $6,000.

I decided it was time to move back to Nova Scotia. The social worker working on my case paid the bill so my

US sponsor wouldn't have to. I had no means to pay at this time. While living in Rochester, I'd bought a 1957 Pontiac and rented a two-bedroom trailer for sixty dollars a month in the same trailer court as my uncle. When my daughter became sick, I decided I would move back to Rochester to be close to her and would only have to take a bus to visit her. While I was hospitalized, my parents came from Nova Scotia to Rochester to visit me. My 1957 Pontiac broke down, so I sold it for fifty dollars. I worked for three and a half years in the States to get an old age pension. I also worked for Bata Shoe Company in the Edgewood neighborhood of Baltimore, Maryland, for six weeks, putting sneakers into the molding machine to affix the soles to the sneakers. After completing the job at Bata Shoe Company and spending two months in the hospital, I decided to move back to Dartmouth, Nova Scotia, Canada. I wasn't back in Nova Scotia for long when I was admitted to the Nova Scotia Hospital in Dartmouth. I spent three months on the N4 ward and then another four months before being transferred to an open ward. I was very depressed, so medical staff began treating me with shock treatments. After about a month, I was discharged. The doctors explained that the reason I was discharged was that I wasn't depressed anymore, but I did need to take medication on a daily basis to prevent getting sick again. I had two children at this time, and my wife, kids, and I resided with my wife's parents. I got a job as a cleaner with the Navy Block for six months. When this term expired, I managed to get another job as a private security guard at an inn, which was a dance hall for bikers. I worked for them for four months. During my work with them, someone put drugs in the drinks, and I ended up going to the hospital again.

When I left the hospital, I went to a restaurant, had a steak, and got really drunk. They called the police, who took me directly back to the Nova Scotia Hospital, where I ended up staying for four months. That was in 1968. In 1969, I bought a two-bedroom house in Dartmouth, not too far from the hospital. My two children had been born in 1962 and 1965. I paid $8,900 for the house. My monthly payments were sixty-two dollars. After owning the house for about six years, I went to sea. I worked on an oil tanker for Imperial Oil, which allowed me to buy a brand-new furnace for the house. I also painted the house, inside and out. When I worked for Imperial Oil I would get laid off a lot, so I decided to go to Ontario to live with my parents. My brother had a house in Oshawa, Ontario, which he sold to my parents. I decided to sell my house and move to Oshawa, Ontario, with my parents. That's when

I drove my 1960 Pontiac off the road on the 401, as I was driving insanely fast.

I was admitted to the hospital in Barrie, Ontario, where I remained for four months and was given injections every two weeks. When I finally got out, I bought a house with a driveway and a 1957 Chevrolet. I also started a cleaning business focused on cleaning offices. I had all the equipment, contracts, and keys to many buildings. My son would help me clean the offices in these buildings. We cleaned floors; vacuumed, polished, and waxed everything; and emptied the garbage bins. We did this for about a year. Then I got another job with Imperial Oil on the big oil tankers. After that I worked as a steward, washing dishes and cleaning rooms and offices. I then sailed for two years.

After leaving the Nova Scotia Hospital in 1967, I went to live with my two sisters, my brother, my father, and my mother in Downsview, Ontario. I got an apartment in the same building as my family, working at Northwestern Hospital in the maintenance department. I checked temperatures with a chart throughout the hospital and presented them to the chief engineer. When a bulb burned out in the operating room, I had to replace it. I cleaned out the fans and fixed plugged toilets with a snake. I also went into the intensive care units and fixed taps. Then they sent me to work in the morgue. My job was to fix the icing coolers and to assist the undertaker. I had to wheel the bodies out to the ice fridges under the supervision of the undertaker. It made my nerves bad, so I quit after four months. The superintendent called my mother, who I was living with at the time, begging her to ask me to come back to work. But my mother said I was sick.

In 1969, I returned from Toronto to Nova Scotia, where I joined the electricians' union. My first job was working for Comstock in Woodside, Dartmouth. I worked with staging, taking down old light fixtures from the ceiling and installing new ones. I threaded conduits and pulled wires through them, bending them with a special pull. The job was finished in four months.

The next job was working for Scotia Square in Halifax, when they were building it in 1969. I was hired as an apprentice and as an electrician's helper in the first year. My job was to thread conduits, pull wires through them to the power boxes, and hook up fixtures outside of the building myself. The largest conduit had a circumference of four inches. We pulled quite thick wires through them to the power boxes. I worked there for four months until the job was finished.

The next job I got was out in Musquodoboit Harbour, where they raised salmon. They had two log houses. My job was to chisel out holes to put power boxes in so that the electricians could wire the boxes for electricity.

The next job I had was wiring houses in Spryfield. It only lasted two months.

I thought if I moved to Toronto I could join the electricians' union, but they said I needed a grade twelve education, and I only had a grade eight education. From 1981 to 1983, I took my grade seven and eight math and English over, and in 1982 to 1983 I went to Dartmouth High School. I got my grade nine and grade ten math. Then in Toronto, from 1982 to 1983, I took grade eleven English and part of my grade twelve English.

In 1970 I returned to Downsview, Ontario, and got a job working for Open Window Bakery as a baker's helper. I saved my money and told my wife to rent the house and move to Toronto, where I got an apartment for her in my mother's building.

I knew my sister's boyfriend worked at Inglo Nickle Mines as a draftsman, so I tried to get a job there. Instead, they sent me to Falconbridge Nickel Mines, where I got a job in the smelter. I was earning $2.65 an hour, and I rented an apartment from them for sixty dollars a month. I bought all-new furniture for a one-bedroom apartment for $600. After three months of saving my money, I moved my wife and two kids to Sudbury, Ontario, which is three hundred miles north of Toronto. I sent my two kids to a Catholic school by bus.

At the smelter, I changed tracks and drove a train for one year. Every morning I had to go into the office, and they put something liquid inside of the gas mask because of the gas fumes. My breathing was so bad after one year that I went to a doctor to get insurance and a leave of absence. I told my wife to sell my furniture for $600, and she got it. I moved back to Nova Scotia and stayed with my wife's mother and father for a month; meanwhile, I gave the tenants in my house thirty days to move. I was getting ninety dollars a week from Falconbridge. I received $125 a week from unemployment insurance.

After going off insurance from Falconbridge and going off unemployment insurance for one year, I was $3,000 behind in house taxes. Welfare paid my house taxes and found me a job by Lake Charles making a trail in the woods across the lake from the Waverly Road for $1.25 an hour. After working in the woods for three weeks clearing out the trail, a guy cut his foot with an axe. I got scared, quit my job, walked across the ice, and started hitchhiking. The manager of a social services program, Mr. Green, picked me up. He said, "You are using tax payers' money!" I told him I would have a job soon. After three weeks, I walked down to the ESSO Refinery from my house in

Woodside, Dartmouth. I was making $800 a month. I gave all my pay to my wife, plus a credit card with a five hundred dollar limit for her to use. I worked three months, with six weeks off.

I then got a job with ESSO working on ships from 1972 to 1974. I was on three different ships: *Imperial Bedford, Imperial Quebec,* and *Imperial Acadia.* As with the refinery, I was working three months on and six weeks off, and my pay was $800. During my second year of sailing, I trained to become a pastry chef. I made homemade breads, rolls, pies, and so on. It was a very different life. I also had to clean the officers' rooms. After that, I sailed with the Coast Guard with the search and rescue department. The ship was in dry dock for about one month. Then I was posted to the *Sir John A. MacDonald,* and we sailed one hundred miles south of the North Pole, breaking ice. To join the ship, we had to board a forty-two-foot sea helicopter, which flew close to three hundred miles. When we finally boarded the ship, which only held four people on board—two passengers and two crew members—my job was as a steward. I cooked, cleaned, and washed dishes. I spent six long years on the ocean with the Coast Guard and Imperial Oil. I was promoted to second cook, and I had a drinking problem I was not aware of. My hands were shaking, and I thought people were looking at me, so I quit and ended up in the Nova Scotia hospital for a month. When I got out, I moved back to Nova Scotia. I had my house for eighteen years. I would go to Ontario, and my wife would draw welfare while I was away.

In 1969 I took a furniture-refinishing course. I refinished many desks, tables, and coffee tables made of oak. I also worked as an electrician for a year. I was in the union at the Canadian Steel plant, making steel for the new bridge being built across Halifax Harbour. I had to sand and grind each steel column and then weld angles on the ends of the rims. I then had to clean up the work area, take the steel columns from the welders, and use the crane to take them to the painters.

The doctor put me on lithium, so I went to Ontario and asked to go to a hospital for the criminally insane in Barrie, Ontario. I asked them to take me off my lithium because I had bad side effects due to drinking alcohol. They put me on modecate injections every two weeks for thirteen years. I passed my four-month course, but I still did not quit drinking alcohol.

I returned to Nova Scotia to start a cleaning business in 1975, as mentioned earlier, but never quit drinking when living in the province. Then I went to Nova Scotia Hospital to see Dr. Holland and take my modecate injection, but I still had a drinking problem of which I was not aware.

In 1976 I returned to Toronto and saw Dr. Jamal for my modecate injection every two weeks. I got a job at Sears for a year, working the back shift. I returned to Nova Scotia in 1979 and worked as a private security guard at the Dartmouth Inn, as I previously mentioned. I had to keep the noise down at the hotel. The bouncer would toss out guys for fighting, and I would have to break up their fights. I once choked a guy and held him until the police arrived. I did that job for four months. The next job I had was with the Canadian Coast Guard with three different ships. Dr. Holland gave Dr. Brown, my family doctor, permission for me to give myself my own thigh injection so I could still sail on the ships. The three ships I sailed on were part of search and rescue, and they were called the *Alert*, the *Louis St. Laurent*, and the *Sir John A. MacDonald*.

I was on the *Alert* for one month at the dry dock at Shelburne, Nova Scotia. The *Sir John A. MacDonald* sailed up to Alaska and then went one hundred miles south of the North Pole breaking ice. We were having trouble, so they flew the whole crew back home. The third ship, the *Louis St. Laurent*, sailed the Gulf of St. Lawrence, breaking ice.

From 1979 to 1980, as previously discussed, I worked for the Canadian Coast Guard. When I got off the *Louis St. Laurent*, my nerves were so bad that I had to go to the Nova Scotia Hospital for a month. My wife filed for divorce; I had three children at the time. One year later, I met someone else named Mary Ella Burns from Porters Lake, and we had a baby boy. We called him Donald Murray Monk. That marriage lasted from 1982 until 1984. I did well with her because I obtained my junior high and grade ten education. My second wife divorced me in 1984 and was still single until she passed away in 2002. Both wives kept their phone numbers unlisted so that I could not talk to my children, and they raised the children well. I was wondering if my second wife was waiting for me to come back to Nova Scotia, so I came back to Nova Scotia in 1991 for ten months and made friends with my second wife. My grandmother was ninety-five years old at the time, and I asked her for tobacco money. My mother drove down from Ontario in 1991. Dr. Holland advised me that I could live close to my second wife but not with her, so I had an apartment on the same street.

When I returned to Toronto in 1991, I went back to work for Open Window Bakery. Someone had broken down the door of the bakery and caused a lot of water damage. I got sick while trying to get the bakery back in order and went to North York Hospital for two weeks. After two weeks, the doctor wrote a note stating that I was able to return to work. I took the note to my boss, but I was drunk, and my boss told me I was fired. So I went upstairs to the lunchroom and busted all the windows. The value of the broken windows was $8,000. The boss arrived at the courthouse with a smile on his face as he was looking at me. He put $8,000 in his bank account. Whoever busted the front door of the bakery and caused the water damage two weeks earlier had been part of an inside job. I got one year's worth of probation due to busting all the windows in the lunchroom and was barred from the bakery for one year.

I finally knew I had a drinking problem. I looked in the newspaper and saw that the New Democratic Party (NDP) government was flying people to the United States for detox for drugs and alcohol. They sent me to Houston, Texas, for thirty-three days, and the NDP government paid $33,000 for the detox program. The detox staff told me that I just made it due to my blood pressure being so high. I returned from Houston on May 21, 1991. They sent a lot of people from Toronto to the United States for detox programs. I quit drinking alcohol two weeks short of ten years. Since 2016, I have only had three beers. I think I am doing very well by not drinking anymore.

When I came back, I had meetings with Bowling Green in Toronto, and they told me about Progress Place, a center for rehabilitation and a transition house. I went for three months and shared accommodations with eleven people. During my stay, I helped with cooking, and the staff gave me my medication. When I went to detox, I did not take my modecate injection with me. My doctors gave me 250 milligrams of Trazodone daily. I applied for a disability support program through welfare and was on a waiting list for nine months. I started to receive disability assistance in 1992.

I arrived in Nova Scotia in July 1991, but then my mother took me back to Toronto, so I had to break my apartment lease. When I returned to Toronto, my disability was waiting for me. Then my grandmother became very sick and had to return back to Nova Scotia.

My grandmother's name was Helen MacKenzie, and she passed away at ninety-seven years old. Once my mother came back from Nova Scotia after my grandmother passed away, I had four credit cards: a MasterCard from TD Trust, a Visa from Royal Bank, a Canadian Tire credit card, and an ESSO credit card. In 1992, I purchased a 1983 Dodge station wagon, for which my mother was mad at me when she arrived back from Nova Scotia.

Bowling Green wanted me to attend Alcoholics Anonymous (AA) and Narcotics Anonymous (NA) at least three times a week. I did not drink for five years. In fact, I couldn't get used to drinking again due to going to detox.

Bowling Green asked me if I could get them more clients for the AA and NA programs. I moved to Montreal in 1994 and got my disability check every month for $728. My room rent was $200 per month. I went to the church for supper every night, so I didn't need to purchase any food.

I had a Montreal health card, and my mother told me to move back to Toronto so that I would not lose my Ontario pension. I was in Montreal for six months, but I came back to Toronto in 1995. I was in debt for $8,000. My car had been crushed in a junkyard in 1993, so I was paying over $300 a month on bills. At the time I rented a basement apartment for $450 per month. Around then I also met a woman from Israel who was five years younger than I was. I met her at Progress Place and asked her to move in with me. She did. But I later found out that she lived in a really nice high-rise apartment building that was well furnished, so I then moved in with her. Her father made her a public guardian trustee so that her finances were handled. We got $516 each for ourselves after we paid the rent. She was on the disability support program welfare. I paid off $8,000 worth of my bills and $1,500 of her bills and saved $1,000 until 2004.

In 1996, we were both having trouble with our nerves. I phoned a doctor and told the doctor to take her off the lithium because she was repeating herself all the time. Even my mother couldn't stand her, but I went to the hospital to be circumcised so I could become Jewish and marry her. I thought about changing religion again for her, and I would go to the synagogue in Toronto on many occasions. I never did convert. While I was living with her, I was invited to a bar mitzvah for her brother's thirteen-year-old son. I went home the night of my circumcision, and the police came to the house again. They said, "You're going to jail." But they told me it was okay for me to take her off her lithium. They took me to jail, and they took her to the hospital. When I went to jail, the doctor at the jail wanted me to take lithium. I refused lithium for three months, and I was very sick. My mother called the nurse up at the jail and told her to give me a modecate injection as I had gotten in the hospital in Barrie, Ontario, back in 1973. My mother thought that injection suited me well. After my mother called the nurse, I got out of jail three weeks later. My girlfriend was out of the hospital; her doctor took her off the lithium and gave her ten milligrams of Olanzapine and sleeping pills. I took some of her medication, went to a doctor, got it prescribed for me, got Trazodone, and went off the injection.

We eventually abandoned her apartment because the television made too much noise. We rented a basement apartment for $600 per month from a Yugoslavian woman. We both got sick again after six months and gave that place up. We both ended up in the hospital. After we got out of the hospital, I went to my mother's, and then we rented a room in Toronto. We were in that room for a year and four months. The room had a bathroom in it. At the end of two years, in 2002, I received a letter from the welfare department stating that I was legally married and had thirty days to appeal. I accepted the fact we were married. My girlfriend received a call from the housing department for an apartment, and I encouraged her to take it, as did the rest of her family. I moved into it with her and went on the lease. We were getting $516 each after the rent was paid.

I rented another room in downtown Toronto after breaking up with my girlfriend. Her dad introduced her to another man whom she later grew to love more than me. This incident broke my heart. From that point on I began to break a lot of things, such as my apartment lease.

I was thinking about living with my mother, but there was no room. My mother and my brother both lived in my mother's apartment. My brother was hard on my mother both mentally and financially. My mother eventually lost her apartment because she was financially providing for my brother and his bad habits. This too broke my heart.

My mother had to move into Toronto housing. This was very upsetting for me. My mother was not the same after all that. She required emergency residence and had no other choice but to turn to Toronto housing.

A week after getting out of jail, my father passed away. I was able to see him before he died. I used to visit my girlfriend's mother and father, and they used to give me groceries and clothing, as her father wore the same size as me.

In 2000 I ended up in jail for six months and asked the jail doctor for the medication malarial. I wasn't doing well at the jail, so the doctor sent me to the Queen Street Hospital for an assessment. The doctor there gave me an injection, and I became high. I was in jail for another week before going back to the hospital, where I met Dr. Brunet. She gave me twenty milligrams of Olanzapine. I refused lithium at this time. I was on probation for two years, and I never missed an appointment with Dr. Brunet.

I moved in with my mother to help with rent; I paid $450 per month. My brother had throat cancer and wanted to move in with my mother as well. He died in 2005. My mother then moved into public housing, and I lost contact with her when I moved downtown—also for $450 per month. I got my meals at the soup kitchen. I had a cell phone. I was then told that I had to move out by the end of the month, and I had nowhere to go but into a hostel.

I walked to my girlfriend's apartment from downtown Toronto, and she would not let me in. I lived on the streets for three weeks with no medication.

The police picked me up and found a hostel for me. What they didn't know was that I was on medication. I became ill, and the police drove me to the hospital that was thirty miles from Toronto, in Whitby, Ontario. While at the hospital, I had nine hundred milligrams of lithium and twenty milligrams of Olanzapine, as well as Ativan for sleeping. I lost all my identification while at the hospital. One of the hospital workers found my bank card and returned it to me. I went to the bank to check my balance. I had $268, which was enough to board a bus for Nova Scotia. So I did.

When I arrived in Nova Scotia, I searched for my son, Donnie. Donnie took care of me for one month. Donnie's girlfriend searched for and found an apartment for me and arranged for me to see a doctor. I was then given medications and began to feel better.

One day my Olanzapine accidentally dropped into the kitchen sink; needless to say, I began getting sick again. I took a break from medications without my doctor's permission, and my mental health worsened. I got into trouble with the law while ill, and the police took me to the East Coast Forensic Psychiatric Hospital. The reason I was admitted was that I had been found "not criminally responsible" (NCR) due to a mental disorder. This was 2005. I had been charged with possession of a weapon and causing a disturbance because I'd been brandishing a large knife at the Dartmouth Bus Terminal while in a manic state with psychiatric symptoms. I was experiencing delusions, and I confronted a bus driver who I thought was wearing an American uniform. I got off the bus and threw the knife into a snowbank. The police had no trouble finding the knife, as they had seen me throw it. I had made no attempt to acquire psychiatric treatment prior to leaving Ontario.

I went to mental health court and, as I said, was found not criminally responsible. I have been in the hospital off and on for eleven years. I was in an apartment for four months, but because of a fire I had to move. I was in a senior building for three and a half years and a group home for two years. As I write this, I am currently back in the hospital. I have had over one hundred shock treatments from 2014 to 2016, and I am now on six hundred milligrams of lithium and fifteen milligrams of Olanzapine. I currently have shock treatment every ten days and am doing better. I soon hope to be out of the hospital for good.

To return to where I left off, back in Nova Scotia, I came to the East Coast Forensic Psychiatric Hospital in 2005. My doctor was Dr. Pottle, and he put me on the same medication for five years. After one year, he discharged me to move into a building for seniors.

From 2001 to 2005 I had three beers, and then I did not drink for another eleven years. Before that eleven years, though, in 2005, I drank a few beers and got in trouble with the law; that was when I was admitted to the East Coast Forensic Psychiatric Hospital. I had no medication in my system and was waiting to see a doctor. Police took me to the hospital to get help. When I finally arrived at the hospital I was assigned Dr. Pottle as my psychiatrist, as mentioned in the previous paragraph. After Dr. Pottle discharged me to the housing for seniors, I lived there for three and a half years and did well. I didn't drink, but I had become manic and had to come back to the hospital. I was forced to give up my place in senior housing due to my illness. After a six-month stay at the hospital, I was again discharged to a small apartment not far from the hospital. I lived there for five months until a student who was also living there left something on the burner and started a fire that burned the house down; that was the apartment I had to leave due to fire. I again had to come back to the hospital, even though I had been doing all right at both apartments. After spending some more time at the hospital, I was again discharged to a group home. I lived at the group home for over two years, until I became manic again. Dr. Pottle readmitted me to the East Coast Forensic Psychiatric Hospital. He started me on nine hundred milligrams of lithium and fifteen milligrams of Olanzapine and sent me back to the group home, but they could not manage me. So I had to go back to the hospital. While at the hospital, we started shock treatments. I don't recall for sure, but I think Dr. Pottle granted me overnights at my brother's. I was very close to my brother. He passed away in 2016. Dr. Brad Kelln, my psychologist, assessed me and said that I was too much of a risk to be out in the community on my own in an apartment, so I came back to the hospital. I lived at the hospital for two years and have been receiving shock treatments ever since every ten days. Dr. Pottle granted me a level four privilege so that I could attend mental health support groups for eight hours. At Connections Club House, I would answer the phones. When I lived in the building for seniors, I went to Connections Monday through Friday for three and half years. I went to Connections when I lived in my apartment too, so I actually went there for six and a half years. I think Dr. Pottle was a good doctor for letting me out of the hospital for that amount of time. I was also on injections every two weeks for thirteen years in Ontario and in other provinces. As previously discussed, I had a drinking problem then. I think I had a good doctor for not using injections on me every two weeks during my time at East Coast Forensic. I want to thank Dr. Brad Kelln for not labeling me as a high-risk patient; this allowed me to get an apartment and go to the group homes. If I'd been labeled as a high-risk patient, I would not have been able to go anywhere. Ms. Ingersoll, my East Coast Forensic case coordinator, would help me get apartments and group homes and also into Connections. She would often take me somewhere for something to eat. As an outing, she once helped me get that apartment in a building for seniors. During those three and a half years when I didn't drink or break the law, Connections was only a ten-minute walk away. Then, as previously mentioned, I stopped taking my medications and became manic, so Dr. Pottle made me come back to the hospital. That's one of the times I had to give up my apartment. He tried me on another kind of medication. After a while, Dr. Pottle let me rent the small one-bedroom apartment that was in the building that caught fire. When it did, I called Ms. Ingersoll to come and get me. She took me back to the hospital. As I've said, I think I had only been out of the hospital for five months at that point. Back at the hospital, Ms. Ingersoll managed to get me into a group home, where I lived for two years. Once again, they couldn't manage me, so Dr. Pottle brought me back to the hospital.

For the last four months, I have had Dr. Brunet as my doctor. I had her in Ontario for five or six years. The older I get, the more manic I seem to become. I receive shock treatments every ten days, and that will be the case for a while. My name is on a list for an old age home along with two or three other people. I may have to wait for six months. I don't know how long I will have to have shock treatments. I am on a pill for borderline diabetes. If I were to drink beer it would interfere with the medication, and I would have to take injections again, which I wouldn't want to do. From April 1991 to my detox in 2001, which is two weeks short of ten years, I didn't drink. Then from 2005 to 2016 I only had three bottles of beer.

In addition to the mental health club passes that Dr. Pottle gave me, which I have been using for the past six years, he also gave me three-hour passes twice a day for use on the hospital grounds when I didn't go to Connections. I would like to thank Dr. Pottle for letting me out of the hospital six and half years out of eleven and for giving me passes to go to Connections while I have been in the hospital. Connections Club House has a gym, where I go sometimes to listen to the country and western music on the radio. I also go to AA meetings at the hospital once a week. Sometimes I need a cane to help me walk and a knee brace for my right knee so I don't fall down. We have a canteen at the hospital and a trust fund. I was two hundred pounds last year, but now I have lost twenty-five pounds. I cut down on eating and have made better food choices to help me with the diabetes. As a result, I have been able to cut down on my diabetic medication. My bowels and urine are working better too. At the top of the hill, just up from the hospital, there is a bus shelter where people can sit down, chat, and smoke. I usually stay there for an hour but have to walk for another hour and then sit again for a short time.

In my wedge in the hospital itself, there are six bedrooms and a large bathroom with showers and tubs and two payphones for patients to use. There is also a sink where you can drink cold water. In my bedroom I have a closet and a bureau to store my belongings as well as a television. As I've mentioned a few times, my brother died last year; well, two weeks ago my sister's husband also died. I am paying her way down from Vancouver, which is four thousand miles away, so I can take her out to eat, and then I will pay her way back to Vancouver. She has many friends who live near the hospital, and she will be coming down this summer to Nova Scotia. She has six children to look after, although I think they are all of working age. My sister also owns two houses, and I think the insurance left money to her. Here at the hospital we have four smoke breaks at nine o'clock in the morning, noon, four o'clock in the evening, and half past five. We have a locker room in the lobby to store our cigarettes. Sometimes a worker will sit and play cards or checkers with me. We have an airing court outside where we go to smoke for fifteen minutes at a time. We can also have three-hour-long smoke breaks at the top of the hill. The smoke breaks at the top of the hill are twice a day, but the winter weather is so cold and dreary that I don't bother going.

I feel good. I am seventy-three years old.

Apparently, the older you are, the harder it is to treat this illness. Dr. Pottle is a good doctor, but he retired from working full-time; he now works just two days a week. This is why I now see Dr. Brunet, who is also a very good doctor. As I've mentioned, I was familiar with her because I had seen her when I lived in Ontario. She left Ontario one year before I did to come to work at the ECFPH in 2004. She is very well educated about shock therapy (ECT), which I continue to receive every ten days. For such a young doctor, she is very bright. My community worker is MaryAnn Ingersoll; as I've mentioned, she helps me find apartments and group homes. She does the same for many other clients living here in ECFPH. She takes me out to eat periodically, which I enjoy very much. When my brother was alive, she would drive sixty miles so I could visit with him. I truly appreciated this. My brother was a florist who owned greenhouses.

When I was twelve years old, as I mentioned near the beginning of this book, I saw the late Hank Williams in concert one year before he died. I was a huge fan and collected several of his albums. Well, I've recently bought a guitar, and I sing his songs when I go to karaoke. I remember his records were the old seventy-eight speed. I had a record player that played them. Then the forty-five speed came out, and after that his albums came out as forty-fives.

I once traveled to the United States and visited the gravesite of John F. Kennedy, who was president of the United States of America from 1961 to 1963. I then went to Long Island, New York, with my brother to visit my uncle for two weeks.

Now, allow me to return to discussing my living arrangements at ECFPH. I presently live in a dayroom or wedge with six rooms, as I started to explain. Each client in my wedge has his own room. The dayrooms are equipped with tables, chairs, sinks, a small fridge, cupboards, and a large bathroom with tubs and shower stalls. We have television with cable. The nursing stations are centrally located in the hospital so that medical staff can observe clients at all times in case of emergency. There are the airing courts outside of the dayrooms where the clients can go smoke a few times a day, as I described, and there is a large kitchen outside of the nursing station where we eat our meals and have coffee. Directly outside of the wedge are tables where we can build puzzles, do arts and crafts, or play cards with other clients. We even have our own laundry room where we each wash our own laundry according to the schedule the nursing staff prepares. Down the hall, there are vending machines where a person can purchase juice, water, or pop. In the same area, there are a number of rooms for treatment programming, exercise, and other interesting things. There is also a special room set up for clients preparing for discharge to go home or to the community. This room is called the DLS or daily living suite. Occupational therapy staff members closely monitor it. Out front, in the main lobby area, is where the administrative offices and reception are located.

Since I have been granted a level four privilege, I am able to walk up the hill to smoke. It is good exercise. This is where clients with full community privileges go to catch the bus to work, school, or outside treatment programs. They also go for their general leisure. I like to go to Connections Club House in Halifax, as I've mentioned a few times. I answer phones, do dishes, and help out wherever they need help. The meals at Connections are delicious. They cost two dollars, which is quite inexpensive for a good, hearty meal. It is a very nice place to socialize and meet people. At the hospital we also have outings. It is especially nice to go on an outing in the summer.

I am doing well these days on my lithium and olanzapine, and I'm taking pain pills for my back. There are times when I am forced to use a cane to help me walk when my back gets sore. I hope to be discharged soon to a complex for seniors where I can live with only two to three other seniors. Dr. Pottle and Dr. Kelln will make the decision about that after assessing my risk factors over a period of time. MaryAnn Ingersoll will find me an appropriate place to live and will supervise that placement. She is taking me out to lunch next week, and I am looking forward to it. The charge nurse on my unit, Shona, is also wonderful. She makes sure I have my medications and reports to the doctors about my health and other things. She cuts my hair and is very helpful. She is a kind and very caring nurse, but she is tough too. She doesn't let anyone pull the wool over her eyes. I consider myself very lucky to have her as my nurse. She keeps me on the straight and narrow, which keeps me from getting depressed and feeling ill.

Résumé for Bruce Monk

Employment History

1956–1961 Royal Canadian Artillery Army Cadets Duties: Target practice, four years of training, drill summer camp, trained in use of firearms, such as submachine guns, rifles, and 9 mm pistols at Camp Aldershot in Kentville, Nova Scotia. Spent six years with merchant navy and army cadets, achieving rank of major.

1961 Canadian Iron, Burnside Park, Dartmouth, Nova Scotia, Duties: Weld tacking, burning steel, fitters helper, assistant crane operator.

1963–1965 New York Central Railroad; enlisted in the United States Army: Classification A1 with selective service, Rochester, New York.

1964–1966 Irving Oil Duties: Worked as an oiler for one year and held the position of steward for two years.

1968   OHIP Building, Toronto, Ontario, Duties: Operated boiler room and air-conditioning units for four hospitals. Worked as general maintenance for a six-year period.

1971   Falconbridge Nickel Mine, Sudbury, Ontario, Duties: Operated train in smelter, changed tracks, cleaned center chutes, dumped ore into furnace to be melted, and transferred ore from center chutes into dump cars attached to engine on track.

1972   Imperial Oil, Dartmouth Marine Slip Duties: Worked two years as a steward, wiper, and second cook.

1974   Monks Cleaning Service Duties: Maintained seven contracts with various Burnside businesses, emptied trashcans, swept, vacuumed, stripped and waxed floors, and maintained keys.

1980–1982 Canadian Coast Guard Duties: Dayworker, steward, and ice breaker.

1991 (4 months) Open Window Bakery, Toronto, Ontario, Duties: Stacker, put loaves of bread on breadboards for baking, removed bread from ovens to cooling racks for preparation for delivery.

1995   Hospital Consultant and Health Care Monks Services Duties: Acted as overseer of staff.

2003   National Specialty Merchandising Corporation (SMC); Monks Retail and Wholesale Services

Education And Training

1969 (9 months) Adult Vocational Training Center Furniture refinishing.

1982–1983 Dartmouth High School Completion of grades seven through ten, math and English.

1992–1993 Monsier Frasier College, Toronto, Ontario. Completion of grade eleven English; studied drama and acting.

Other Skills: Threading conduit with threading machine, operating jackhammers and concrete drills used to drill holes in cement, using carpenter's level, safely operating bench saws, wood drills, hand saws, hack saws, and drivers.

Volunteer Services

1991–1995 Worked for the Conservative Party

1995–2000 Worked for the Liberal Party PQ of Quebec